THE JAZZ SINGER

ISBN 0-88188-510-X
(previously ISBN 0-89524-130-7)

HAL LEONARD
PUBLISHING
CORPORATION

Home Office: National Sales Office:
960 East Mark Street   8112 West Bluemound Road
Winona MN 55987   Milwaukee WI 53213

ACAPULCO

Words by NEIL DIAMOND
Music by NEIL DIAMOND & DOUG RHONE

AMAZED AND CONFUSED

Words by NEIL DIAMOND
Music by NEIL DIAMOND & RICHARD BENNETT

Some-bod-y's wait-in' on the Riv-er Jor-dan.
Some-bod-y's call-in' on the Riv-er Jor-dan.

Some-bod-y's wait-in' on the oth-er side.
Some-bod-y's call-in' from the oth-er side.
I cast my stones on the way

AMERICA

Words and Music by
NEIL DIAMOND

Moderately bright

Far,   we've been trav - el - ing far,___

with - out___ a   home,___

Ev-'ry time___ that flag's ___ un-furled, ___ they're com-ing to A-

mer - i - ca. Got a dream to take___ them there.

They're com-ing to A - mer - i - ca. Got a dream___ they've come___

___ to share. They're com-ing to A - mer - i - ca.

HAVAH NAGILAH

Traditional
Adaptation by NEIL DIAMOND

Start slowly and accelerate to end

Ha - vah _____ na - gi - lah, Ha - vah _____ na - gi - lah,

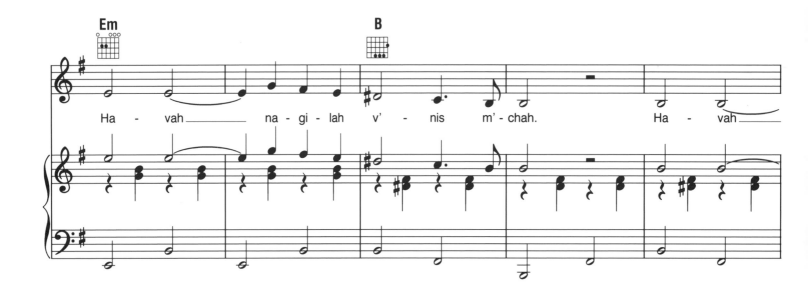

Ha - vah _____ na - gi - lah v' - nis m' - chah. Ha - vah

_____ na - gi - lah, Ha - vah _____ na - gi - lah, Ha - vah _____

HELLO AGAIN

Words by NEIL DIAMOND
Music by NEIL DIAMOND & ALAN LINDGREN

Moderately slow

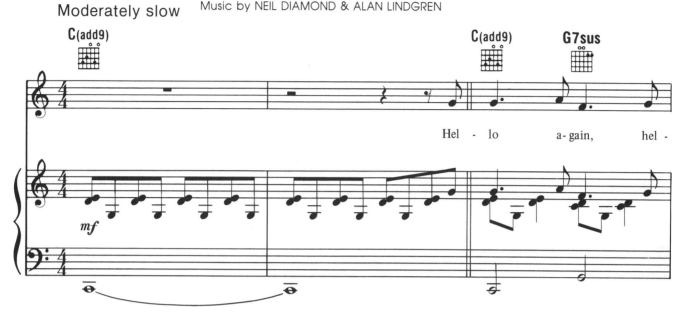

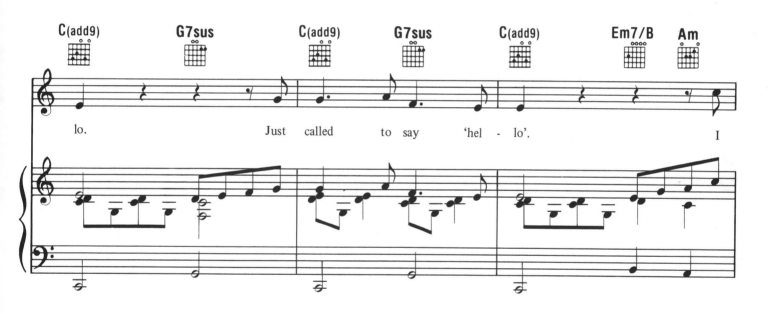

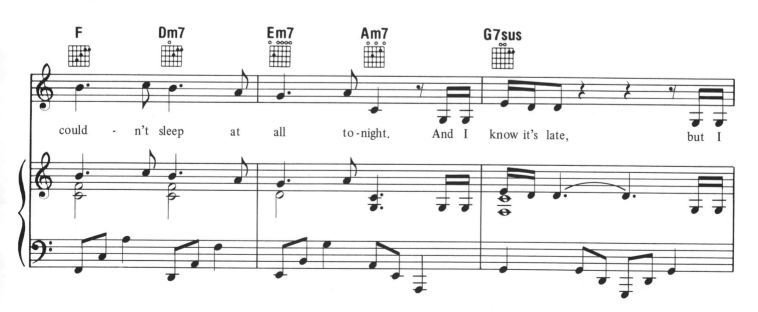

ADON OLOM

Traditional
Adaptation by NEIL DIAMOND & URI FRENKEL

HINE MAH TOV

Traditional
Adaptation by NEIL DIAMOND

HEY LOUISE

Words and Music by
NEIL DIAMOND & GILBERT BECAUD

Brightly (in 2)

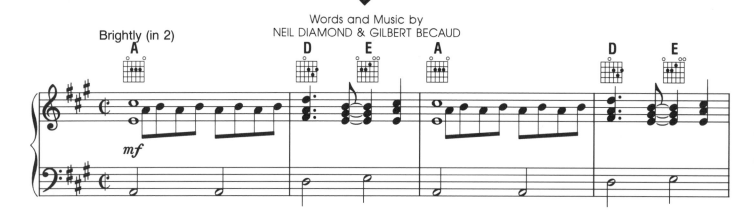

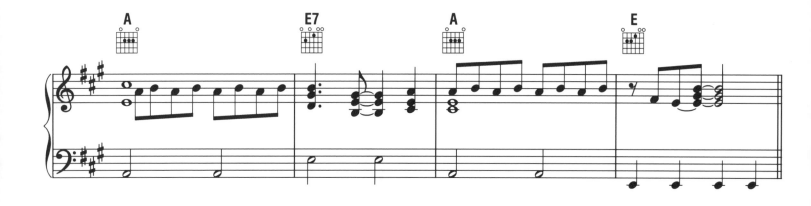

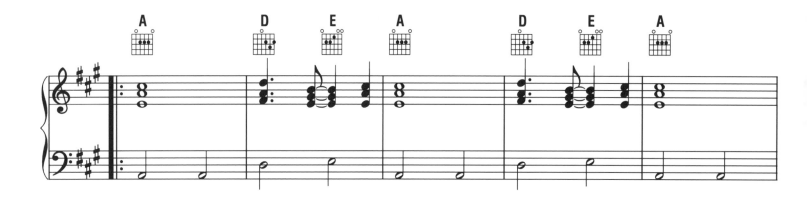

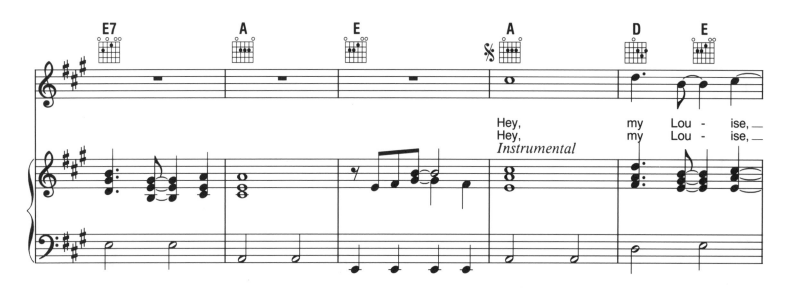

Hey,   my   Lou—   ise, ___
Hey,   my   Lou—   ise, ___
Instrumental

JERUSALEM

Words and Music by
NEIL DIAMOND

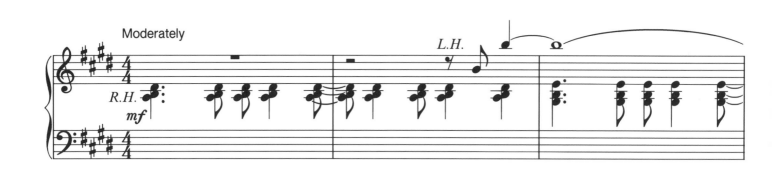

KOL NIDRE

Traditional
Adaptation by NEIL DIAMOND & URI FRENKEL

Quickly

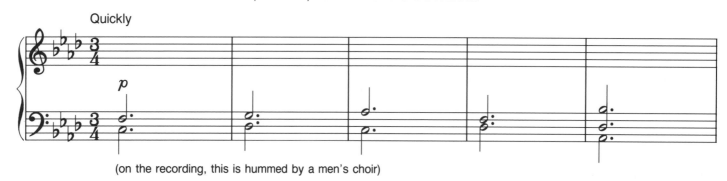

(on the recording, this is hummed by a men's choir)

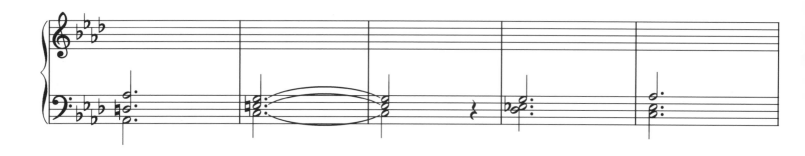

Slowly and very freely

Kol Nid - re_____ ve - e - so - re_____ va - cha - ro -

LOVE ON THE ROCKS

Words and Music by
NEIL DIAMOND & GILBERT BECAUD

Moderately slow Ballad

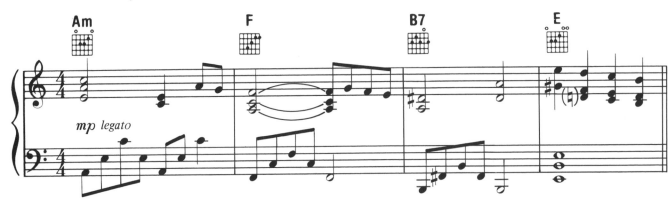

mp legato

Love on the rocks   ain't no sur-prise.

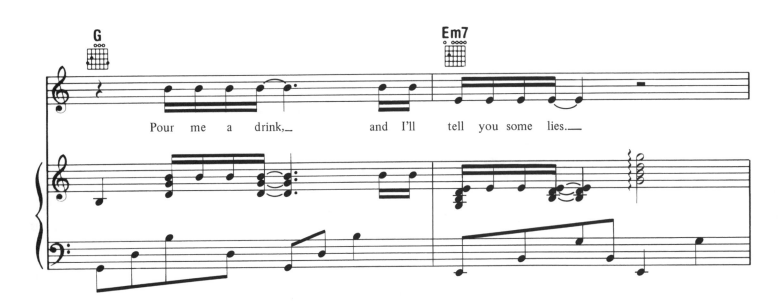

Pour me a drink,_ and I'll tell you some lies._

ON THE ROBERT E. LEE

Words and Music by
NEIL DIAMOND & GILBERT BECAUD

Hey, look at the way she's wav-in' her sail. It's a

SHABBAT SHALOM

Traditional words
Music by URI FRENKEL

SONGS OF LIFE

Words and Music by
NEIL DIAMOND & GILBERT BECAUD

YOU BABY

Words and Music by
NEIL DIAMOND

SUMMERLOVE

Words and Music by
NEIL DIAMOND & GILBERT BECAUD

Sum - mer love ___ made it right.
sum - mer love ___ made us one.